# THE CARTOON BOOK

# EDITED BY
# CINDY GARNER

Newport House
100 Via Estrada, Suite P
Laguna Hills, CA 92653
714/770-8323

To Alan and Erick,
The best of men


MEN: THE CARTOON BOOK

Newport House gratefully acknowledges the following for permission to reprint cartoons: Randy Glasbergen, P.O. Box 736, Sherburne, NY 13460, who contributed the back cover cartoon and the first and seventeenth cartoons in the book, copyright 1974, 1980, 1981, 1982, 1983, 1984, 1985, 1986, 1987, 1988, 1989 by Randy Glasbergen. Harley Schwadron, P.O. Box 1347, Ann Arbor, MI 48106, who contributed the next fifteen   cartoons in this book, copyright 1980, 1981, 1982, 1983, 1984, 1985,1986, 1987, 1988, 1989, 1990 by Harley Schwadron. Saturday Evening Post, which contributed all of the other cartoons in this work, copyright 1968, 1972, 1977, 1978, 1979, 1980, 1981, 1982, 1983, 1984, 1985, 1986, 1987, 1988, 1989, 1990 by Saturday Evening Post. Requests for reprint rights should be addressed to those listed above.

First Newport House edition: July 1990

ISBN: 0-939515-44-X

*"Got any stinkweed?"*

*"Miss Weltzschatenz, I accidentally answered the phone myself. Am I in?"*

*"Separate clouds, please."*

"As my first male secretary, your duties
do not include reminding me that 'I've
Come A Long Way, Baby.'"

*"Sure it's lonely at the top, but don't forget, Jason, no one liked you before you made it to the top either."*

"Drive it away Alden. Tell it one of your jokes."

"I'm moving into Mother's house, and she's moving
in here to 'shape you up.'"

"I checked, but Mr. Fogarty is not in any of his usual hiding places."

"Frankly, I don't have much confidence in his diet book either."

"Would you like me to read that back so you can hear how silly it sounds?"

"We'll be starting you at the bottom, Mr. Herkimer.
Manicure my toenails."

"This is a hostile corporate takeover offer.
Just because we're divorced is no reason we
still can't be enemies, Norman!"

"Welcome aboard, Mr. Dahlberg. I've decided
to hire you as my 'Boy Friday.'"

*"I kissed you on the cheek before I left for work this morning.
Does that count as foreplay?"*

"He's a grouch and a hypocrite."

*"Don't pay any attention, Monica—*
*He's just upset because you're sitting in his chair."*

"I'd better be getting home now,
Herbert—my interest rate is dropping."

"What item in the budget have I overlooked?"

"Hi, Judy, can we talk, or is this a bad time?"

*"Everything I do lately seems to irritate you."*

"There goes the picture tube. Well, Mabel,
how have you been the past few years?"

"For years she's been telling me I'm the greatest.
Last night I happened to ask her the greatest <u>what</u>..."

"You are a leader of men. You are brave,
handsome, strong and popular with the ladies.
It has your weight wrong, too."

*"Howard?"*

*"When I think of all the years you let me blame the kids for this mess...!"*

*"I saved a bundle by fixing the brakes myself. Just remember, if you want to stop, you have to press hard on the radio dial."*

*"But enough about me—let's talk about football."*

*"He hasn't paid attention to me since he
started hitting that little stone in the hole."*

*"Strange...I suddenly have this overwhelming urge to go home and pick my socks up off the bedroom floor!"*

"Let me get this straight: you need space, you feel we're going in different directions, and you want to see other people. Does this mean you won't marry me?"

*"So, what seems to be the problem?"*

"Of course, I remember the last time
I took you out! It was in 1975, right after the
Cowboys beat Minnesota 17-14..."

*"Fred and I are celebrating our 35th baseball season together."*

"Raise your feet. I want to clean the stadium."

"The X-rays indicate you're crying on the inside."

*"And the time he won a trip to Hawaii for two...he went twice."*

"This is the first time he's taken me anywhere in five years."

"Yes, Dear, of course, Dear. Yes, Dear..."

"My mom scrubbed floors night and day
to help me get ahead. So, now that I own the
company, I'm putting her on straight days."

*"No, Mother, I'm <u>sure</u> Al wasn't out running around with other women while I was away."*

*"Well, for one thing, he's very possessive."*

"Where on earth does all your grocery money go?"

"Just pay the bill, Harold. Must you be so competitive?"

*"Admit it Harold...we're lost!"*

"And do you, Harley, promise to love,
honor, cherish, stop smoking, lose 20 pounds,
eat more wholesome foods..."

*"Say, did you have that broken arm when
I left for work this morning?"*

"You shouldn't have to do that, dear.
Where's that lazy son of yours?"

*"Well, then, will you marry me next after Herb?"*

"Mr. Nevele, our interior decorator, suggests
that we put you in the attic, dear."

"Your wife understands you a little—
she knows you're here."

"George, can't you ever relax?"

*"Edgar's need for entertainment is at a bare minimum."*

*"Me take you for granted? You kidding...
and lose out on a sure thing?"*

*"He never takes anything seriously."*

☐ EVERYTHING MEN KNOW ABOUT WOMEN by Dr. Alan Francis. The perfect gift for all your friends! Have them read the front of the book...the back of the book...and then let them look inside...The book is absolutely empty!                                                                                    5 for $14.75

☐ EVERYTHING MEN KNOW ABOUT ROMANCE by Dr. Alan Francis. This book tells you everything men know about listening to women, talking to women, and sharing feelings with women.Another blank masterpiece!                                                                                            5 for $14.75

☐ MEN: THE CARTOON BOOK                                                                            $4.95

☐ CONVERSATIONALLY SPEAKING by Alan Garner, M.A. "Want to be a popular conversationalist? Reading Alan Garner's book will help." —Norman Vincent Peale                           $5.95

☐ HOW TO ATTRACT THE OPPOSITE SEX by Alan Garner, M.A. In this tape, the million-selling author teaches and demonstrates how to establish rapport with the opposite sex, double your confidence, and avoid rejection-producing behavior.                                                                $9.95

☐ CASH IN ON TAX LIEN CERTIFICATES by Cindy Garner and Marcia Hootman, Ph.D. Counties in 30 states issue tax lien certificates paying 16-50% on your money. Find out how you can make big money by buying up these certificates.                                                                      $19.95

---

The first four books listed are at your local bookstore. All books listed can be obtained from Newport House, 100 Via Estrada, Suite P, Laguna Hills, CA 92653 by using this coupon.

Please send me the books I have checked. I am enclosing $ _____ (Please add $1 to cover postage. Calif. residents add tax.) Send check or money order - no COD.

Name _____

Address _____

City _____ State _____ Zip _____

*Allow 4 weeks for delivery.*